45 Raspberry Recipes for Home

By: Kelly Johnson

Table of Contents

Breakfast and Brunch:

- Raspberry Pancakes
- Raspberry Smoothie Bowl
- Raspberry Almond Oatmeal
- Raspberry Chia Seed Pudding
- Raspberry French Toast

Drinks:

- Raspberry Lemonade
- Raspberry Mint Iced Tea
- Raspberry Mojito
- Raspberry Lime Spritzer
- Raspberry Smoothie

Appetizers and Snacks:

- Raspberry Brie Bites
- Raspberry Salsa
- Raspberry Bruschetta
- Raspberry Guacamole
- Raspberry Hummus

Salads:

- Raspberry Spinach Salad
- Grilled Chicken Raspberry Salad
- Quinoa Raspberry Salad
- Raspberry Walnut Salad
- Smoked Salmon Raspberry Salad

Main Courses:

- Raspberry Glazed Salmon
- Raspberry Balsamic Chicken

- Pork Tenderloin with Raspberry Sauce
- Raspberry BBQ Ribs
- Raspberry Teriyaki Stir-Fry

Desserts:

- Raspberry Cheesecake
- Raspberry Chocolate Tart
- Raspberry Mousse
- Raspberry Sorbet
- Raspberry Coconut Panna Cotta

Baked Goods:

- Raspberry Almond Scones
- Raspberry Streusel Muffins
- Raspberry White Chocolate Cookies
- Raspberry Swirl Brownies
- Raspberry Lemon Bars

Ice Cream and Frozen Treats:

- Raspberry Swirl Ice Cream
- Chocolate Raspberry Popsicles
- Raspberry Frozen Yogurt
- Raspberry Sorbet Floats
- Raspberry Ice Cream Sandwiches

Jams and Preserves:

- Homemade Raspberry Jam
- Raspberry Balsamic Reduction
- Spicy Raspberry Sauce
- Raspberry Lemon Curd
- Raspberry Compote

Breakfast and Brunch:

Raspberry Pancakes

Ingredients:

- 1 cup all-purpose flour
- 2 tablespoons sugar
- 1 teaspoon baking powder
- 1/2 teaspoon baking soda
- 1/4 teaspoon salt
- 1 cup buttermilk
- 1 large egg
- 2 tablespoons unsalted butter, melted
- 1 teaspoon vanilla extract
- 1 cup fresh raspberries
- Maple syrup for serving

Instructions:

In a large mixing bowl, whisk together the flour, sugar, baking powder, baking soda, and salt.

In a separate bowl, whisk together the buttermilk, egg, melted butter, and vanilla extract.

Pour the wet ingredients into the dry ingredients and gently fold until just combined. Be careful not to overmix; it's okay if there are a few lumps.

Gently fold in the fresh raspberries into the batter.

Heat a griddle or non-stick skillet over medium heat and lightly grease with cooking spray or butter.

For each pancake, ladle about 1/4 cup of batter onto the griddle. Cook until bubbles form on the surface, then flip and cook until the other side is golden brown.

Repeat until all the batter is used, keeping the cooked pancakes warm in a low oven.

Serve the raspberry pancakes warm, topped with additional fresh raspberries and a drizzle of maple syrup.

Enjoy your delightful and fruity breakfast!

Raspberry Smoothie Bowl

Ingredients:

- 1 cup frozen raspberries
- 1 frozen banana, sliced
- 1/2 cup plain Greek yogurt
- 1/4 cup almond milk (or any milk of your choice)
- 1 tablespoon chia seeds
- 1 tablespoon honey or maple syrup (optional, for sweetness)
- Toppings: Fresh raspberries, sliced banana, granola, shredded coconut, and a sprinkle of chia seeds

Instructions:

In a blender, combine the frozen raspberries, frozen banana slices, Greek yogurt, almond milk, and chia seeds.
Blend on high speed until smooth and creamy. Add honey or maple syrup if additional sweetness is desired, then blend again to combine.
Pour the smoothie into a bowl.
Arrange the toppings on the smoothie bowl. Use fresh raspberries, sliced banana, granola, shredded coconut, and a sprinkle of chia seeds for a colorful and textured bowl.
Feel free to get creative with the arrangement of toppings, making your smoothie bowl visually appealing.
Serve immediately and enjoy this nutritious and vibrant Raspberry Smoothie Bowl!

Tip: You can customize the toppings based on your preferences and add other fruits, nuts, or seeds for added variety and nutritional benefits.

Raspberry Almond Oatmeal

Ingredients:

- 1 cup old-fashioned rolled oats
- 2 cups milk (dairy or plant-based)
- 1/2 cup fresh raspberries
- 2 tablespoons sliced almonds
- 1 tablespoon almond butter
- 1 tablespoon honey or maple syrup (optional, for sweetness)
- 1/2 teaspoon almond extract
- Pinch of salt
- Additional raspberries and sliced almonds for garnish

Instructions:

In a medium saucepan, combine the rolled oats and milk. Bring to a simmer over medium heat.
Once the mixture starts to simmer, reduce the heat to medium-low and cook, stirring frequently, until the oats are tender and the mixture has thickened, about 5-7 minutes.
Stir in the fresh raspberries, sliced almonds, almond butter, almond extract, and a pinch of salt. Continue to cook for an additional 2-3 minutes, or until the raspberries are slightly softened.
If desired, add honey or maple syrup for sweetness and adjust according to your taste preferences. Stir well to combine.
Remove the oatmeal from the heat and let it sit for a minute to thicken further.
Serve the Raspberry Almond Oatmeal in bowls, garnished with additional fresh raspberries and sliced almonds.
Enjoy this wholesome and delicious breakfast that combines the nutty flavor of almonds with the sweet and tart taste of fresh raspberries!

Raspberry Chia Seed Pudding

Ingredients:

- 1/4 cup chia seeds
- 1 cup almond milk (or any milk of your choice)
- 1 tablespoon maple syrup or honey
- 1/2 teaspoon vanilla extract
- 1/2 cup fresh raspberries
- Additional raspberries and mint leaves for garnish

Instructions:

In a bowl, combine chia seeds, almond milk, maple syrup (or honey), and vanilla extract. Stir well to ensure the chia seeds are evenly distributed.

Allow the mixture to sit for about 5 minutes, then stir again to prevent clumping. Repeat this process a couple more times over the next 15-20 minutes until the chia seeds absorb the liquid and start to thicken.

Once the mixture has thickened, gently fold in fresh raspberries. You can lightly crush some of the raspberries to release their juices for added flavor.

Cover the bowl and refrigerate the chia seed pudding for at least 4 hours or preferably overnight to allow the chia seeds to fully absorb the liquid.

Before serving, give the pudding a good stir. If it's too thick, you can add a little more almond milk to reach your desired consistency.

Spoon the Raspberry Chia Seed Pudding into serving bowls or jars.

Garnish with additional fresh raspberries and mint leaves for a burst of color and freshness.

Enjoy this delightful and nutritious Raspberry Chia Seed Pudding as a healthy breakfast or snack!

Raspberry French Toast

Ingredients:

For the French Toast:

- 4 slices of thick bread (brioche or challah works well)
- 2 large eggs
- 1/2 cup milk
- 1 teaspoon vanilla extract
- 1/2 teaspoon ground cinnamon
- Butter for cooking

For the Raspberry Compote:

- 1 cup fresh raspberries
- 2 tablespoons sugar
- 1 tablespoon water
- 1 teaspoon lemon juice

Optional Toppings:

- Powdered sugar
- Maple syrup
- Fresh mint leaves

Instructions:

French Toast:

In a shallow dish, whisk together the eggs, milk, vanilla extract, and ground cinnamon.
Dip each slice of bread into the egg mixture, ensuring both sides are well-coated.
Heat a skillet or griddle over medium heat and add a knob of butter.
Cook the soaked bread slices until golden brown on both sides, about 3-4 minutes per side. Repeat for each slice.

Raspberry Compote:

In a small saucepan, combine fresh raspberries, sugar, water, and lemon juice.
Bring the mixture to a simmer over medium heat, stirring occasionally.

Once the raspberries have softened and the sauce has thickened slightly (about 5 minutes), remove from heat.
Use a fork to mash some of the raspberries if you prefer a chunkier compote.

Assembly:

Place the French toast slices on serving plates.
Spoon the warm Raspberry Compote generously over the French toast.
Optionally, dust with powdered sugar and garnish with fresh mint leaves.
Serve immediately with maple syrup on the side if desired.

Enjoy this indulgent Raspberry French Toast for a delightful breakfast or brunch!

Drinks:

Raspberry Lemonade

Ingredients:

- 1 cup fresh raspberries
- 1 cup freshly squeezed lemon juice (about 4-5 lemons)
- 1 cup granulated sugar (adjust according to taste)
- 4 cups cold water
- Ice cubes
- Lemon slices and fresh raspberries for garnish
- Mint leaves for garnish (optional)

Instructions:

Make Raspberry Puree:
- In a blender, puree the fresh raspberries until smooth.
- Strain the raspberry puree through a fine-mesh sieve to remove seeds, collecting the smooth liquid in a bowl.

Prepare Simple Syrup:
- In a small saucepan, combine the sugar with 1 cup of water. Heat over medium heat, stirring until the sugar is completely dissolved. Remove from heat and let it cool.

Mix Lemonade Base:
- In a large pitcher, combine the freshly squeezed lemon juice, raspberry puree, and simple syrup. Stir well to combine.

Add Cold Water:
- Pour 4 cups of cold water into the pitcher. Adjust the water quantity based on your desired sweetness and tartness.

Chill the Lemonade:
- Refrigerate the raspberry lemonade for at least 1-2 hours to allow the flavors to meld.

Serve:
- Fill glasses with ice cubes and pour the chilled raspberry lemonade over the ice.

Garnish:
- Garnish each glass with lemon slices, fresh raspberries, and mint leaves if desired.

Stir and Enjoy:
- Give the raspberry lemonade a gentle stir before serving. Enjoy this refreshing and vibrant drink on a hot day!

Feel free to adjust the sugar and lemon ratios to suit your taste preferences. This Raspberry Lemonade is perfect for picnics, parties, or simply as a delightful thirst-quencher.

Raspberry Mint Iced Tea

Ingredients:

- 4 cups water
- 4 black tea bags
- 1/2 cup fresh raspberries
- 1/4 cup fresh mint leaves, plus extra for garnish
- 1/2 cup granulated sugar (adjust to taste)
- Ice cubes
- Lemon slices for garnish (optional)

Instructions:

Brew the Tea:
- Bring 4 cups of water to a boil in a saucepan.
- Add the tea bags to the boiling water and let them steep for about 5 minutes. Remove the tea bags and discard.

Make Raspberry Mint Syrup:
- In a separate saucepan, combine fresh raspberries, mint leaves, and sugar.
- Mash the raspberries with a fork or spoon as they heat up.
- Simmer the mixture over low heat for 5-7 minutes until the sugar is dissolved, and the raspberries release their juices.

Strain and Cool:
- Strain the raspberry mint syrup through a fine-mesh sieve, collecting the liquid in a bowl. Discard the solids.
- Allow the syrup to cool to room temperature.

Combine Tea and Syrup:
- In a pitcher, combine the brewed tea and raspberry mint syrup. Stir well to mix.

Chill:
- Refrigerate the raspberry mint iced tea until it's thoroughly chilled, about 2 hours.

Serve Over Ice:
- Fill glasses with ice cubes and pour the chilled raspberry mint iced tea over the ice.

Garnish:
- Garnish each glass with a sprig of fresh mint and lemon slices if desired.

Stir and Enjoy:
- Give the iced tea a gentle stir before sipping. Enjoy the refreshing combination of raspberry and mint flavors!

Feel free to customize the sweetness by adjusting the amount of sugar in the syrup. This Raspberry Mint Iced Tea is a delightful beverage for warm days or as a flavorful accompaniment to any meal.

Raspberry Mojito

Ingredients:

- 10 fresh mint leaves, plus extra for garnish
- 1/2 lime, cut into wedges
- 2 tablespoons granulated sugar (adjust to taste)
- 1/2 cup fresh raspberries
- 2 ounces white rum
- 1 cup ice cubes
- 1/2 cup club soda
- Fresh raspberries and lime slices for garnish

Instructions:

Muddle Mint, Lime, and Sugar:
- In a glass, place the fresh mint leaves, lime wedges, and sugar. Use a muddler or the back of a spoon to gently muddle the ingredients, releasing the mint and lime flavors.

Add Raspberries:
- Add the fresh raspberries to the glass and muddle them with the mint, lime, and sugar mixture.

Add Ice and Rum:
- Fill the glass with ice cubes.
- Pour the white rum over the ice.

Top with Club Soda:
- Top off the glass with club soda. Stir gently to combine all the ingredients.

Garnish:
- Garnish the Raspberry Mojito with additional fresh raspberries, lime slices, and a sprig of mint.

Serve and Enjoy:
- Serve the Raspberry Mojito immediately while it's refreshingly cold.

Adjust Sweetness:
- Taste the mojito and adjust the sweetness by adding more sugar if necessary.

Sip and Relax:
- Sip and enjoy this fruity and minty Raspberry Mojito for a perfect, summery treat.

Feel free to customize the recipe by adding more or less sugar, adjusting the amount of mint, or experimenting with different proportions based on your personal taste preferences. Cheers!

Raspberry Lime Spritzer

Ingredients:

- 1 cup fresh raspberries
- 4 limes, juiced
- 1/4 cup granulated sugar (adjust to taste)
- 2 cups sparkling water
- Ice cubes
- Fresh mint leaves for garnish
- Lime slices for garnish

Instructions:

Make Raspberry Lime Syrup:
- In a blender, puree the fresh raspberries until smooth.
- Strain the raspberry puree through a fine-mesh sieve to remove seeds, collecting the smooth liquid in a bowl.
- In the same bowl, combine the raspberry puree with freshly squeezed lime juice and granulated sugar. Stir well until the sugar is dissolved.

Prepare Glasses:
- Fill glasses with ice cubes to your liking.

Add Raspberry Lime Syrup:
- Pour the raspberry lime syrup over the ice in each glass.

Top with Sparkling Water:
- Pour sparkling water over the raspberry lime syrup, filling each glass to the top.

Stir Gently:
- Gently stir the mixture to combine the flavors.

Garnish:
- Garnish each glass with fresh mint leaves and lime slices for a burst of freshness.

Serve Immediately:
- Serve the Raspberry Lime Spritzer immediately for maximum fizziness.

Adjust Sweetness:
- Taste the spritzer and adjust the sweetness by adding more sugar if desired.

Enjoy:
- Enjoy this sparkling and fruity Raspberry Lime Spritzer as a refreshing beverage on a hot day!

Feel free to experiment with the ratio of raspberry lime syrup to sparkling water to suit your taste preferences. This spritzer is perfect for any occasion, whether it's a picnic, brunch, or a simple relaxing afternoon.

Raspberry Smoothie

Ingredients:

- 1 cup fresh or frozen raspberries
- 1 ripe banana
- 1/2 cup Greek yogurt
- 1/2 cup almond milk (or any milk of your choice)
- 1 tablespoon honey or maple syrup (optional, for sweetness)
- 1/2 teaspoon vanilla extract
- Ice cubes (if using fresh raspberries)
- Chia seeds or flaxseeds for added nutrition (optional)

Instructions:

Prepare Ingredients:
- If using fresh raspberries, wash them thoroughly. If using frozen raspberries, let them thaw for a few minutes.

Blend:
- In a blender, combine the raspberries, ripe banana, Greek yogurt, almond milk, honey or maple syrup, and vanilla extract.

Add Ice Cubes (if needed):
- If you want a colder and thicker smoothie, add a handful of ice cubes to the blender.

Blend Until Smooth:
- Blend all the ingredients until you achieve a smooth and creamy consistency.

Taste and Adjust:
- Taste the smoothie and adjust the sweetness by adding more honey or maple syrup if necessary.

Optional: Add Chia Seeds or Flaxseeds:
- For added nutrition, consider blending in a tablespoon of chia seeds or flaxseeds.

Serve Immediately:
- Pour the raspberry smoothie into glasses and serve immediately.

Garnish (Optional):
- Garnish with a few whole raspberries on top for a decorative touch.

Enjoy:
- Enjoy this refreshing and nutritious Raspberry Smoothie as a quick and delicious breakfast or snack.

Feel free to customize this smoothie by adding other fruits, greens, or seeds according to your taste preferences and nutritional goals. It's a great way to start your day with a burst of fruity goodness!

Appetizers and Snacks:

Raspberry Brie Bites

Ingredients:

- 1 sheet puff pastry, thawed
- 1/2 cup raspberry preserves
- 8 ounces Brie cheese, cut into small cubes
- 1/4 cup chopped walnuts or pecans (optional)
- Fresh raspberries for garnish
- Fresh thyme leaves for garnish (optional)
- Honey for drizzling

Instructions:

Preheat Oven:
- Preheat your oven according to the puff pastry package instructions.

Prepare Puff Pastry:
- Roll out the thawed puff pastry sheet on a lightly floured surface.

Cut Pastry Squares:
- Using a knife or a square cookie cutter, cut the puff pastry into small squares (about 2 inches by 2 inches).

Assemble Bites:
- Place each puff pastry square in a mini muffin tin, gently pressing them down to form small cups.

Add Raspberry Preserves:
- Spoon a small amount of raspberry preserves into the bottom of each puff pastry cup.

Add Brie Cubes:
- Place a cube of Brie on top of the raspberry preserves in each cup.

Optional: Add Nuts:
- If using, sprinkle chopped walnuts or pecans on top of the Brie in each cup.

Bake:
- Bake the raspberry Brie bites in the preheated oven according to the puff pastry package instructions or until the pastry is golden brown and the Brie is melted.

Garnish:

- Remove from the oven and let them cool for a minute. Garnish each bite with a fresh raspberry and a few thyme leaves if desired.

Drizzle with Honey:
- Just before serving, drizzle the raspberry Brie bites with honey for an extra touch of sweetness.

Serve Warm:
- Serve the raspberry Brie bites warm as an elegant appetizer for parties or gatherings.

These Raspberry Brie Bites are a delightful combination of sweet and savory flavors, making them a perfect addition to your appetizer spread.

Raspberry Salsa

Ingredients:

- 1 cup fresh raspberries, coarsely chopped
- 1 cup cherry tomatoes, diced
- 1/2 cup red onion, finely chopped
- 1/4 cup fresh cilantro, chopped
- 1 jalapeño, finely diced (seeds removed for less heat, if desired)
- 1 tablespoon fresh lime juice
- 1 teaspoon honey
- Salt and pepper to taste
- Tortilla chips for serving

Instructions:

Prepare Ingredients:
- Coarsely chop the fresh raspberries and dice the cherry tomatoes.

Combine Ingredients:
- In a medium-sized bowl, combine the chopped raspberries, diced cherry tomatoes, finely chopped red onion, diced jalapeño, and chopped cilantro.

Add Lime Juice and Honey:
- Drizzle the fresh lime juice and honey over the mixture.

Season with Salt and Pepper:
- Season the salsa with salt and pepper according to your taste preferences.

Mix Well:
- Gently toss all the ingredients together until well combined. Be careful not to crush the raspberries too much; you want the salsa to have a chunky texture.

Chill (Optional):
- If time allows, refrigerate the raspberry salsa for about 30 minutes to let the flavors meld. This step is optional but enhances the overall taste.

Serve:
- Serve the raspberry salsa in a bowl alongside tortilla chips.

Enjoy:
- Enjoy this vibrant and fruity Raspberry Salsa as a refreshing appetizer or a unique topping for grilled chicken or fish.

Feel free to customize the salsa by adding diced avocado or mango for an extra layer of flavor.

This versatile salsa adds a burst of color and taste to your table, making it perfect for picnics, barbecues, or any festive occasion.

Raspberry Bruschetta

Ingredients:

- 1 French baguette, sliced into 1/2-inch thick rounds
- 1 cup fresh raspberries, coarsely chopped
- 1/2 cup goat cheese or cream cheese
- 2 tablespoons balsamic glaze
- 1/4 cup fresh basil, thinly sliced
- 1 tablespoon honey
- Olive oil for drizzling
- Salt and pepper to taste

Instructions:

Toast the Baguette:
- Preheat the oven to 375°F (190°C). Arrange the baguette slices on a baking sheet and drizzle with olive oil. Toast in the oven for 8-10 minutes or until golden brown and crisp.

Prepare Raspberry Topping:
- In a bowl, gently mix the coarsely chopped raspberries with balsamic glaze, thinly sliced basil, honey, salt, and pepper. Toss until well combined.

Spread Cheese on Toast:
- Once the baguette slices are toasted, spread a layer of goat cheese or cream cheese on each slice.

Top with Raspberry Mixture:
- Spoon the raspberry mixture generously over the cheese-covered baguette slices.

Drizzle with Balsamic Glaze:
- Drizzle a bit more balsamic glaze over the top for added richness and flavor.

Garnish:
- Garnish the raspberry bruschetta with additional fresh basil leaves.

Serve:
- Arrange the Raspberry Bruschetta on a serving platter and serve immediately.

Enjoy:
- Enjoy this elegant and fruity twist on classic bruschetta as a delightful appetizer for parties, brunch, or any special occasion.

Feel free to experiment with the toppings by adding a sprinkle of chopped nuts, such as walnuts or pistachios, or a drizzle of honey for extra sweetness. The combination of flavors makes this Raspberry Bruschetta a crowd-pleaser.

Raspberry Guacamole

Ingredients:

- 3 ripe avocados, peeled, pitted, and mashed
- 1 cup fresh raspberries, coarsely chopped
- 1/2 cup red onion, finely diced
- 1 jalapeño, finely minced (seeds removed for less heat, if desired)
- 1/4 cup fresh cilantro, chopped
- 2 tablespoons lime juice
- Salt and pepper to taste
- Tortilla chips for serving

Instructions:

Prepare Avocados:
- In a bowl, mash the ripe avocados with a fork until you achieve your desired guacamole consistency.

Add Raspberries:
- Gently fold the coarsely chopped raspberries into the mashed avocados.

Mix in Ingredients:
- Add the finely diced red onion, minced jalapeño, chopped cilantro, and lime juice to the bowl.

Season:
- Season the guacamole with salt and pepper according to your taste preferences.

Gently Combine:
- Gently fold all the ingredients together until well combined. Be cautious not to crush the raspberries completely; you want them to provide a burst of sweetness in each bite.

Taste and Adjust:
- Taste the guacamole and adjust lime, salt, or pepper if needed.

Chill (Optional):
- For enhanced flavors, you can refrigerate the raspberry guacamole for about 30 minutes.

Serve:
- Serve the Raspberry Guacamole in a bowl with tortilla chips on the side.

Enjoy:
- Enjoy this unique and flavorful guacamole as a delicious dip for gatherings, parties, or as a refreshing snack.

The addition of raspberries adds a delightful sweetness and vibrant color to the classic guacamole. Feel free to customize by adding diced tomatoes, extra cilantro, or a splash of hot sauce for an extra kick!

Salads:

Raspberry Spinach Salad

Ingredients:

For the Salad:

- 6 cups fresh baby spinach, washed and dried
- 1 cup fresh raspberries
- 1/2 cup feta cheese, crumbled
- 1/4 cup red onion, thinly sliced
- 1/4 cup sliced almonds, toasted
- Optional: Grilled chicken or shrimp for added protein

For the Raspberry Vinaigrette:

- 1/3 cup fresh raspberries
- 2 tablespoons balsamic vinegar
- 1 tablespoon Dijon mustard
- 1 tablespoon honey
- 1/4 cup extra-virgin olive oil
- Salt and pepper to taste

Instructions:

For the Raspberry Vinaigrette:

Prepare Raspberry Puree:
- In a blender, blend the fresh raspberries until smooth. Strain the puree through a fine-mesh sieve to remove seeds, collecting the smooth liquid in a bowl.

Whisk Dressing:
- In a small bowl, whisk together the raspberry puree, balsamic vinegar, Dijon mustard, and honey.

Emulsify with Olive Oil:
- While whisking continuously, slowly drizzle in the extra-virgin olive oil to emulsify the dressing.

Season:

- Season the vinaigrette with salt and pepper to taste. Adjust sweetness or acidity if desired.

For the Salad:

Assemble Salad:
- In a large salad bowl, combine the fresh baby spinach, raspberries, crumbled feta cheese, sliced red onion, and toasted sliced almonds.

Add Protein (Optional):
- If desired, add grilled chicken or shrimp to make the salad a complete meal.

Drizzle with Raspberry Vinaigrette:
- Just before serving, drizzle the raspberry vinaigrette over the salad. Toss gently to coat evenly.

Serve:
- Serve the Raspberry Spinach Salad immediately, ensuring each bite is coated with the delicious vinaigrette.

Enjoy:
- Enjoy this vibrant and nutritious salad as a refreshing side or a light and satisfying main course.

Feel free to customize the salad with additional toppings like avocado, cucumber, or your favorite nuts. The raspberry vinaigrette adds a sweet and tangy flavor, complementing the freshness of the spinach and raspberries.

Grilled Chicken Raspberry Salad

Ingredients:

For the Grilled Chicken:

- 4 boneless, skinless chicken breasts
- 2 tablespoons olive oil
- 2 cloves garlic, minced
- 1 teaspoon dried thyme
- Salt and black pepper, to taste

For the Raspberry Vinaigrette:

- 1 cup fresh raspberries
- 3 tablespoons balsamic vinegar
- 1/4 cup extra-virgin olive oil
- 1 tablespoon honey
- Salt and black pepper, to taste

For the Salad:

- Mixed salad greens (lettuce, spinach, arugula, etc.)
- 1 cup fresh raspberries
- 1 cup cherry tomatoes, halved
- 1 cucumber, sliced
- 1/2 red onion, thinly sliced
- 1/2 cup feta cheese, crumbled
- 1/4 cup chopped fresh basil

Instructions:

1. Grilled Chicken:

- In a bowl, mix olive oil, minced garlic, dried thyme, salt, and black pepper to create the marinade.

- Coat chicken breasts with the marinade and let them marinate for at least 30 minutes.
- Preheat the grill to medium-high heat.
- Grill the chicken breasts for 6-8 minutes per side or until fully cooked and grill marks appear.
- Let the chicken rest for a few minutes before slicing.

2. Raspberry Vinaigrette:

- In a blender, combine fresh raspberries, balsamic vinegar, olive oil, honey, salt, and black pepper.
- Blend until smooth.
- Strain the mixture to remove seeds, if desired.

3. Salad Assembly:

- In a large salad bowl, combine mixed greens, fresh raspberries, cherry tomatoes, cucumber, red onion, and feta cheese.
- Add the sliced grilled chicken on top.
- Drizzle the raspberry vinaigrette over the salad.
- Toss the salad gently to coat everything with the dressing.
- Sprinkle chopped fresh basil on top for an extra burst of flavor.

4. Serve:

- Divide the salad among serving plates.
- Optionally, garnish with additional feta cheese and fresh basil.
- Serve immediately and enjoy your Grilled Chicken Raspberry Salad!

This salad offers a delightful combination of grilled chicken, sweet raspberries, and a tangy vinaigrette, making it a refreshing and satisfying dish. Feel free to customize the salad with your favorite additional ingredients or adjust the dressing according to your taste preferences.

Quinoa Raspberry Salad

Ingredients:

- 1 cup quinoa, rinsed
- 2 cups water or vegetable broth
- 1 cup fresh raspberries
- 1/4 cup sliced almonds, toasted
- 1/4 cup crumbled feta cheese
- 2 tablespoons fresh mint leaves, chopped
- 2 tablespoons fresh basil leaves, chopped

For the Dressing:

- 3 tablespoons olive oil
- 2 tablespoons balsamic vinegar
- 1 tablespoon honey
- Salt and pepper to taste

Instructions:

Cook Quinoa:
- In a medium saucepan, bring the water or vegetable broth to a boil.
- Stir in the quinoa, reduce the heat to low, cover, and simmer for 15-20 minutes, or until the quinoa is cooked and the liquid is absorbed.
- Remove from heat and let it cool to room temperature.

Prepare Dressing:
- In a small bowl, whisk together the olive oil, balsamic vinegar, honey, salt, and pepper until well combined. Set aside.

Assemble Salad:
- In a large mixing bowl, combine the cooked quinoa, fresh raspberries, toasted almonds, crumbled feta cheese, chopped mint leaves, and chopped basil leaves.
- Pour the dressing over the salad and toss gently to coat all the ingredients evenly.

Serve:
- Transfer the quinoa raspberry salad to a serving platter or individual plates.

- Garnish with additional fresh raspberries, almonds, feta cheese, mint leaves, and basil leaves if desired.
- Serve immediately as a refreshing side dish or a light meal.

This quinoa raspberry salad is packed with flavor and nutrients, making it a perfect dish for summer gatherings or as a nutritious lunch option. Feel free to customize the salad by adding your favorite ingredients like avocado, cucumber, or grilled chicken for extra protein. Enjoy!

Raspberry Walnut Salad

Ingredients:

- 6 cups mixed salad greens (lettuce, spinach, arugula, etc.)
- 1 cup fresh raspberries
- 1/2 cup chopped walnuts, toasted
- 1/2 cup crumbled feta cheese
- 1/4 red onion, thinly sliced
- 1/4 cup balsamic vinaigrette dressing
- Salt and pepper to taste

Instructions:

Prepare Salad Greens:
- Wash and thoroughly dry the mixed salad greens. Place them in a large salad bowl.

Add Raspberries and Walnuts:
- Gently wash the raspberries and add them to the salad greens.
- In a dry skillet over medium heat, toast the chopped walnuts for a few minutes until they become fragrant. Be careful not to burn them. Add the toasted walnuts to the salad.

Incorporate Feta and Red Onion:
- Crumble the feta cheese over the salad.
- Thinly slice the red onion and add it to the salad.

Dress the Salad:
- Drizzle the balsamic vinaigrette dressing over the salad.
- Toss the salad gently to ensure all ingredients are well coated with the dressing.

Season and Serve:
- Season the salad with salt and pepper to taste.
- Serve immediately as a refreshing side dish or add grilled chicken or salmon for a complete meal.

This Raspberry Walnut Salad is a delightful combination of sweet, tart, and crunchy elements. It's perfect for a light lunch, a side dish for dinner, or as a refreshing salad for a summer picnic. Enjoy!

Smoked Salmon Raspberry Salad

Ingredients:

- 6 cups mixed salad greens (arugula, spinach, or your favorite greens)
- 4 ounces smoked salmon, thinly sliced
- 1 cup fresh raspberries
- 1/2 cup crumbled goat cheese
- 1/4 cup red onion, thinly sliced
- 1/4 cup chopped walnuts, toasted
- 2 tablespoons extra-virgin olive oil
- 1 tablespoon balsamic vinegar
- 1 teaspoon Dijon mustard
- Salt and pepper, to taste

Instructions:

Prepare Salad Greens:
- Wash and dry the mixed salad greens thoroughly. Place them in a large salad bowl.

Add Smoked Salmon and Raspberries:
- Lay the thinly sliced smoked salmon over the salad greens.
- Gently wash the raspberries and add them to the salad.

Incorporate Goat Cheese and Red Onion:
- Crumble the goat cheese over the salad.
- Thinly slice the red onion and sprinkle it over the salad.

Toast Walnuts:
- In a dry skillet over medium heat, toast the chopped walnuts for a few minutes until fragrant. Be cautious not to burn them. Add the toasted walnuts to the salad.

Prepare Dressing:
- In a small bowl, whisk together the extra-virgin olive oil, balsamic vinegar, Dijon mustard, salt, and pepper to create the dressing.

Dress the Salad:
- Drizzle the dressing over the salad.
- Toss the salad gently to coat all the ingredients with the dressing.

Serve:
- Arrange the salad on plates or a serving platter.
- Serve immediately as a light and flavorful meal.

This Smoked Salmon Raspberry Salad is a wonderful combination of savory smoked salmon, sweet raspberries, and tangy goat cheese. The toasted walnuts add a delightful crunch, and the dressing ties everything together for a delicious and elegant salad. Enjoy!

Main Courses:

Raspberry Glazed Salmon

Ingredients:

- 4 salmon fillets
- Salt and pepper, to taste
- 1 cup fresh raspberries
- 2 tablespoons balsamic vinegar
- 2 tablespoons honey
- 1 tablespoon Dijon mustard
- 2 tablespoons olive oil
- Chopped fresh parsley for garnish (optional)

Instructions:

Preheat Oven:
- Preheat your oven to 400°F (200°C).

Season Salmon:
- Season the salmon fillets with salt and pepper to taste.

Make Raspberry Glaze:
- In a blender or food processor, combine the raspberries, balsamic vinegar, honey, and Dijon mustard. Blend until smooth.
- Strain the raspberry mixture through a fine-mesh sieve into a bowl to remove seeds, extracting as much liquid as possible.

Sear Salmon:
- In an oven-safe skillet, heat olive oil over medium-high heat.
- Sear the salmon fillets, skin side down, for about 2 minutes or until the skin is golden and crisp.

Glaze Salmon:
- Spoon the raspberry glaze over the seared side of the salmon fillets.

Bake:
- Transfer the skillet to the preheated oven and bake for about 8-10 minutes or until the salmon is cooked through and flakes easily with a fork.

Garnish and Serve:
- Remove from the oven and garnish with chopped fresh parsley, if desired.
- Serve the raspberry glazed salmon fillets with additional glaze on top.

This Raspberry Glazed Salmon recipe offers a perfect balance of sweet and savory flavors with the vibrant taste of fresh raspberries. It's a delightful and impressive dish that's relatively quick to prepare. Enjoy!

Raspberry Balsamic Chicken

Ingredients:

- 4 boneless, skinless chicken breasts
- Salt and pepper, to taste
- 1 cup fresh raspberries
- 1/4 cup balsamic vinegar
- 2 tablespoons honey
- 2 cloves garlic, minced
- 2 tablespoons olive oil
- Fresh basil, chopped, for garnish (optional)

Instructions:

Season Chicken:
- Season the chicken breasts with salt and pepper to taste.

Make Raspberry Balsamic Glaze:
- In a blender or food processor, combine the raspberries, balsamic vinegar, honey, and minced garlic. Blend until smooth.
- Strain the raspberry mixture through a fine-mesh sieve into a bowl to remove seeds, extracting as much liquid as possible.

Sear Chicken:
- In a large skillet, heat olive oil over medium-high heat.
- Sear the chicken breasts for about 4-5 minutes on each side or until golden brown and cooked through.

Add Glaze:
- Pour the raspberry balsamic glaze over the seared chicken breasts in the skillet.

Simmer:
- Reduce the heat to low and let the chicken simmer in the glaze for an additional 2-3 minutes, allowing the flavors to meld.

Garnish and Serve:
- Garnish with chopped fresh basil, if desired.
- Serve the Raspberry Balsamic Chicken over rice, quinoa, or with your favorite side dishes.

This Raspberry Balsamic Chicken recipe brings together the tangy sweetness of raspberries and the rich depth of balsamic vinegar for a flavorful and elegant dish. Enjoy!

Pork Tenderloin with Raspberry Sauce

Ingredients:

- 1 1/2 pounds pork tenderloin
- Salt and black pepper, to taste
- 2 tablespoons olive oil
- 1 cup fresh raspberries
- 1/4 cup raspberry preserves
- 2 tablespoons balsamic vinegar
- 2 tablespoons honey
- 2 cloves garlic, minced
- 1 teaspoon Dijon mustard
- Fresh parsley, chopped, for garnish (optional)

Instructions:

Preheat Oven:
- Preheat your oven to 400°F (200°C).

Season Pork Tenderloin:
- Season the pork tenderloin with salt and black pepper.

Sear Pork:
- In an ovenproof skillet, heat olive oil over medium-high heat. Sear the pork tenderloin on all sides until browned.

Bake:
- Transfer the skillet to the preheated oven and bake for about 15-20 minutes or until the internal temperature of the pork reaches 145°F (63°C).

Make Raspberry Sauce:
- In a small saucepan, combine raspberries, raspberry preserves, balsamic vinegar, honey, minced garlic, and Dijon mustard.
- Cook over medium heat, stirring occasionally, until the raspberries break down, and the sauce thickens slightly.

Slice Pork and Serve:
- Allow the pork to rest for a few minutes before slicing.
- Serve the sliced pork tenderloin with the raspberry sauce drizzled over the top.

Garnish and Serve:
- Garnish with chopped fresh parsley, if desired.

This Pork Tenderloin with Raspberry Sauce is a delightful combination of savory and sweet flavors. The raspberry sauce adds a burst of fruity goodness to the succulent pork. Enjoy!

Raspberry BBQ Ribs

Ingredients:

- 2 racks of baby back ribs
- Salt and black pepper, to taste
- 1 cup fresh raspberries
- 1 cup barbecue sauce
- 1/4 cup raspberry preserves
- 2 tablespoons apple cider vinegar
- 2 tablespoons soy sauce
- 2 cloves garlic, minced
- 1 teaspoon Dijon mustard
- 1/2 teaspoon smoked paprika
- 1/2 teaspoon onion powder
- 1/4 teaspoon cayenne pepper (adjust to taste)
- Fresh parsley or cilantro, chopped, for garnish (optional)

Instructions:

Preheat Oven:
- Preheat your oven to 275°F (135°C).

Prepare Ribs:
- Remove the membrane from the back of the ribs and season both sides with salt and black pepper.

Wrap in Foil:
- Wrap each rack of ribs tightly in aluminum foil and place them on a baking sheet.

Bake:
- Bake the ribs in the preheated oven for 2.5 to 3 hours or until they are tender.

Make Raspberry BBQ Sauce:
- In a saucepan, combine raspberries, barbecue sauce, raspberry preserves, apple cider vinegar, soy sauce, minced garlic, Dijon mustard, smoked paprika, onion powder, and cayenne pepper.
- Cook over medium heat, stirring occasionally, until the raspberries break down, and the sauce thickens slightly.

Grill or Broil:

- Preheat your grill or broiler.
- Remove the ribs from the foil and brush them generously with the raspberry BBQ sauce.

Grill or Broil Ribs:
- Grill or broil the ribs for about 5-7 minutes per side, basting with additional sauce, until they develop a caramelized crust.

Garnish and Serve:
- Garnish with chopped fresh parsley or cilantro, if desired.
- Slice the ribs between the bones and serve with extra raspberry BBQ sauce on the side.

These Raspberry BBQ Ribs are a sweet and tangy twist on classic barbecue ribs, making them a perfect addition to your cookout or family dinner. Enjoy!

Raspberry Teriyaki Stir-Fry

Ingredients:

For the Teriyaki Sauce:

- 1/2 cup soy sauce
- 1/4 cup rice vinegar
- 2 tablespoons honey
- 1 tablespoon sesame oil
- 1 tablespoon cornstarch
- 1 teaspoon minced ginger
- 1 teaspoon minced garlic

For the Stir-Fry:

- 1 pound boneless, skinless chicken breasts, thinly sliced
- 2 tablespoons vegetable oil
- 1 cup broccoli florets
- 1 red bell pepper, thinly sliced
- 1 yellow bell pepper, thinly sliced
- 1 cup snap peas, trimmed
- 1 carrot, julienned
- 1 cup fresh raspberries
- Cooked rice or noodles for serving
- Sesame seeds and chopped green onions for garnish

Instructions:

Prepare Teriyaki Sauce:
- In a small bowl, whisk together soy sauce, rice vinegar, honey, sesame oil, cornstarch, minced ginger, and minced garlic. Set aside.

Stir-Fry Chicken:
- Heat 1 tablespoon of vegetable oil in a wok or large skillet over medium-high heat.
- Add sliced chicken and stir-fry until browned and cooked through. Remove chicken from the pan and set aside.

Cook Vegetables:
- In the same pan, add another tablespoon of oi .
- Add broccoli, bell peppers, snap peas, and julienned carrot. Stir-fry until the vegetables are crisp-tender.

Combine and Add Sauce:
- Return the cooked chicken to the pan with the vegetables.
- Pour the prepared teriyaki sauce over the chicken and vegetables.
- Toss everything together until well-coated and heated through.

Add Raspberries:
- Gently fold in fresh raspberries, being careful not to crush them. Cook for an additional 1-2 minutes until the raspberries are heated but still intact.

Serve:
- Serve the Raspberry Teriyaki Stir-Fry over cooked rice or noodles.
- Garnish with sesame seeds and chopped green onions.

This Raspberry Teriyaki Stir-Fry offers a delightful combination of savory and sweet flavors, making it a colorful and tasty dish. Enjoy!

Desserts:

Raspberry Cheesecake

Ingredients:

For the Crust:

- 1 1/2 cups graham cracker crumbs
- 1/4 cup melted butter
- 2 tablespoons sugar

For the Cheesecake Filling:

- 24 ounces cream cheese, softened
- 1 cup sugar
- 3 large eggs
- 1 teaspoon vanilla extract
- 1/2 cup sour cream
- 1/2 cup raspberry puree (made by blending fresh raspberries and straining out the seeds)

For the Raspberry Swirl:

- 1/2 cup raspberry puree
- 2 tablespoons sugar

For Garnish:

- Fresh raspberries
- Mint leaves

Instructions:

    Preheat Oven:
- Preheat your oven to 325°F (163°C). Grease a 9-inch springform pan with butter.

    Prepare Crust:
- In a bowl, combine graham cracker crumbs, melted butter, and sugar.

- Press the mixture into the bottom of the prepared springform pan to form the crust.

Prepare Raspberry Swirl:
- In a small bowl, mix 1/2 cup raspberry puree with 2 tablespoons of sugar. Set aside.

Prepare Cheesecake Filling:
- In a large mixing bowl, beat the softened cream cheese until smooth.
- Add sugar and continue to beat until well combined.
- Add eggs one at a time, beating well after each addition.
- Mix in vanilla extract, sour cream, and 1/2 cup raspberry puree until smooth.

Assemble Cheesecake:
- Pour the cheesecake filling over the crust in the springform pan.
- Spoon dollops of the raspberry swirl mixture on top of the cheesecake batter.

Swirl the Raspberry Mixture:
- Use a knife or toothpick to swirl the raspberry mixture into the cheesecake batter, creating a marbled effect.

Bake:
- Bake in the preheated oven for about 50-60 minutes or until the center is set and the edges are lightly browned.

Cool and Chill:
- Allow the cheesecake to cool in the pan for about 15 minutes, then run a knife around the edge to loosen it.
- Chill the cheesecake in the refrigerator for at least 4 hours or overnight.

Garnish and Serve:
- Before serving, garnish the top of the cheesecake with fresh raspberries and mint leaves.

Enjoy this Raspberry Cheesecake as a delightful and fruity dessert!

Raspberry Chocolate Tart

Ingredients:

For the Chocolate Tart Crust:

- 1 1/2 cups chocolate cookie crumbs
- 1/3 cup melted butter
- 2 tablespoons sugar

For the Chocolate Ganache:

- 1 cup semi-sweet chocolate chips
- 1/2 cup heavy cream

For the Raspberry Filling:

- 2 cups fresh raspberries
- 1/4 cup sugar
- 1 tablespoon cornstarch
- 1 tablespoon water

For Garnish:

- Fresh mint leaves
- Additional raspberries

Instructions:

Preheat Oven:
- Preheat your oven to 350°F (175°C).

Prepare Chocolate Tart Crust:
- In a bowl, mix together chocolate cookie crumbs, melted butter, and sugar until well combined.
- Press the mixture into the bottom and up the sides of a tart pan to form the crust.
- Bake the crust in the preheated oven for about 8-10 minutes. Allow it to cool completely.

Prepare Chocolate Ganache:
- In a heatproof bowl, combine the chocolate chips and heavy cream.

- Microwave in 30-second intervals, stirring each time until the chocolate is melted and smooth.
- Pour the chocolate ganache into the cooled tart crust and spread it evenly. Let it set.

Prepare Raspberry Filling:
- In a saucepan, combine raspberries, sugar, cornstarch, and water.
- Cook over medium heat, stirring gently until the raspberries break down and the mixture thickens.
- Remove from heat and let it cool slightly.

Assemble the Tart:
- Spoon the raspberry filling over the chocolate ganache layer in the tart crust.

Chill:
- Place the tart in the refrigerator to chill for at least 2 hours, allowing it to set.

Garnish and Serve:
- Before serving, garnish the tart with fresh mint leaves and additional raspberries.

Serve:
- Slice and serve the Raspberry Chocolate Tart. Enjoy!

This Raspberry Chocolate Tart combines the rich and indulgent flavors of chocolate with the bright and fruity taste of fresh raspberries for a delightful dessert.

Raspberry Mousse

Ingredients:

- 2 cups fresh raspberries
- 1/2 cup sugar
- 2 tablespoons water
- 1 tablespoon lemon juice
- 1 tablespoon gelatin
- 3 tablespoons cold water
- 1 1/2 cups heavy cream
- 1/2 cup powdered sugar
- Fresh raspberries for garnish (optional)
- Mint leaves for garnish (optional)

Instructions:

Prepare Raspberry Puree:
- In a blender or food processor, puree the fresh raspberries until smooth.
- Strain the puree through a fine mesh sieve into a bowl to remove seeds, collecting the raspberry juice. Discard the seeds.

Make Raspberry Sauce:
- In a saucepan, combine the raspberry puree, sugar, 2 tablespoons water, and lemon juice.
- Heat the mixture over medium heat, stirring occasionally until the sugar dissolves and the mixture comes to a simmer.
- Remove from heat and let it cool.

Prepare Gelatin:
- In a small bowl, sprinkle the gelatin over 3 tablespoons of cold water. Let it sit for a few minutes to bloom.

Dissolve Gelatin:
- Microwave the bloomed gelatin for about 10 seconds or until it's completely dissolved. Be careful not to overheat.

Combine Gelatin and Raspberry Sauce:
- Stir the dissolved gelatin into the cooled raspberry sauce. Mix well.

Whip Heavy Cream:
- In a separate bowl, whip the heavy cream and powdered sugar until stiff peaks form.

Combine Raspberry Mixture and Whipped Cream:

- Gently fold the raspberry mixture into the whipped cream until well combined. Be careful not to deflate the whipped cream.

Chill:
- Spoon the raspberry mousse into serving glasses or bowls.
- Refrigerate for at least 2-3 hours or until the mousse is set.

Garnish and Serve:
- Before serving, garnish with fresh raspberries and mint leaves if desired.

Enjoy:
- Serve and enjoy the delicious Raspberry Mousse!

This Raspberry Mousse is a light and airy dessert with the sweet and tangy flavor of fresh raspberries. It's perfect for a refreshing treat, and the vibrant color makes it an elegant addition to any table.

Raspberry Sorbet

Ingredients:

- 3 cups fresh or frozen raspberries
- 1 cup granulated sugar
- 1 cup water
- 1 tablespoon fresh lemon juice

Instructions:

Prepare Simple Syrup:
- In a small saucepan, combine the sugar and water. Heat over medium heat, stirring occasionally, until the sugar is completely dissolved. This creates a simple syrup.

Blend Raspberries:
- In a blender or food processor, blend the raspberries until smooth.

Strain Raspberry Puree:
- If you prefer a smoother sorbet, strain the raspberry puree through a fine-mesh sieve to remove seeds. This step is optional.

Combine Raspberry Puree and Simple Syrup:
- In a mixing bowl, combine the raspberry puree with the simple syrup. Add fresh lemon juice and mix well.

Chill Mixture:
- Refrigerate the mixture for at least 2 hours or until thoroughly chilled.

Churn in Ice Cream Maker:
- Pour the chilled raspberry mixture into an ice cream maker and churn according to the manufacturer's instructions.

Transfer to Container:
- Transfer the churned sorbet into a lidded container.

Freeze:
- Freeze the sorbet for an additional 4-6 hours or until firm.

Serve:
- Scoop the raspberry sorbet into bowls or cones.

Enjoy:
- Enjoy the refreshing and fruity goodness of homemade Raspberry Sorbet!

This Raspberry Sorbet is a delightful and cooling dessert, perfect for a hot day or a sweet treat after a meal. The vibrant color and intense raspberry flavor make it a crowd-pleaser, and it's relatively easy to make at home.

Raspberry Coconut Panna Cotta

Ingredients:

For the Panna Cotta:

- 2 cups coconut milk
- 1/2 cup sugar
- 1 teaspoon vanilla extract
- 2 teaspoons gelatin powder
- 2 tablespoons cold water

For the Raspberry Sauce:

- 1 cup fresh or frozen raspberries
- 2 tablespoons sugar
- 1 tablespoon lemon juice

Instructions:

Prepare Gelatin:
- In a small bowl, sprinkle the gelatin over cold water. Let it sit for a few minutes to bloom.

Warm Coconut Milk:
- In a saucepan, heat the coconut milk and sugar over medium heat. Stir until the sugar is dissolved. Add the vanilla extract and continue to heat until the mixture is warm but not boiling.

Dissolve Gelatin:
- Add the bloomed gelatin to the warm coconut milk mixture. Stir until the gelatin is completely dissolved.

Pour into Molds:
- Remove the saucepan from heat. Allow the mixture to cool slightly. Pour the coconut milk mixture into individual serving molds or glasses.

Chill:
- Place the molds or glasses in the refrigerator and let the panna cotta set for at least 4 hours or until firm.

Prepare Raspberry Sauce:

- In a small saucepan, combine raspberries, sugar, and lemon juice. Cook over medium heat, stirring occasionally until the raspberries break down and the sauce thickens slightly. Remove from heat and let it cool.

Serve:
- Once the panna cotta is set, spoon the raspberry sauce over the top.

Garnish (Optional):
- Garnish with additional fresh raspberries, mint leaves, or shredded coconut if desired.

Enjoy:
- Serve and enjoy this delicious Raspberry Coconut Panna Cotta!

This dessert combines the creamy coconut flavor of the panna cotta with the sweet and tart taste of raspberry sauce, creating a delightful and elegant treat.

Baked Goods:

Raspberry Almond Scones

Ingredients:

- 2 cups all-purpose flour
- 1/3 cup granulated sugar
- 1 tablespoon baking powder
- 1/2 teaspoon salt
- 1/2 cup unsalted butter, cold and cut into small pieces
- 1/2 cup sliced almonds
- 1 cup fresh raspberries
- 1/2 cup milk
- 1 teaspoon almond extract
- 1 teaspoon vanilla extract
- Optional: Powdered sugar for dusting

Instructions:

Preheat Oven:
- Preheat your oven to 400°F (200°C). Line a baking sheet with parchment paper.

Mix Dry Ingredients:
- In a large bowl, whisk together the flour, sugar, baking powder, and salt.

Cut in Butter:
- Add the cold, diced butter to the dry ingredients. Use a pastry cutter or your fingers to cut the butter into the flour until the mixture resembles coarse crumbs.

Add Almonds and Raspberries:
- Stir in the sliced almonds. Gently fold in the fresh raspberries, being careful not to crush them too much.

Combine Wet Ingredients:
- In a separate bowl, mix together the milk, almond extract, and vanilla extract.

Combine Wet and Dry Ingredients:
- Pour the wet ingredients into the dry ingredients and stir until just combined. Be cautious not to overmix.

Form Dough:

- Turn the dough out onto a lightly floured surface. Gently knead it a few times until it comes together. Pat the dough into a circle about 1 inch thick.

Cut Scones:
- Use a floured round cutter or a sharp knife to cut out scones from the dough. Place them on the prepared baking sheet, leaving some space between each.

Bake:
- Bake in the preheated oven for about 15-18 minutes or until the scones are golden brown.

Cool:
- Allow the scones to cool on a wire rack.

Optional: Dust with Powdered Sugar:
- Once cooled, you can dust the scones with powdered sugar if desired.

Serve:
- Serve the Raspberry Almond Scones with your favorite tea or coffee.

These scones are a delightful combination of the nutty flavor from almonds and the sweet-tartness of fresh raspberries. Enjoy this treat for breakfast or as a lovely addition to your afternoon tea.

Raspberry Streusel Muffins

Ingredients:

For the Streusel Topping:

- 1/4 cup all-purpose flour
- 2 tablespoons granulated sugar
- 2 tablespoons unsalted butter, cold and cut into small pieces

For the Muffins:

- 1 and 1/2 cups all-purpose flour
- 1/2 cup granulated sugar
- 2 teaspoons baking powder
- 1/4 teaspoon salt
- 1/2 cup unsalted butter, melted and cooled
- 2/3 cup milk
- 1 large egg
- 1 teaspoon vanilla extract
- 1 and 1/2 cups fresh raspberries

Instructions:

1. Preheat Oven:

- Preheat your oven to 375°F (190°C). Line a muffin tin with paper liners or grease it lightly.

2. Prepare Streusel Topping:

- In a small bowl, combine the streusel topping ingredients - flour, sugar, and cold butter pieces. Use a fork or your fingers to mix until crumbly. Set aside.

3. Mix Dry Ingredients:

- In a large bowl, whisk together the flour, sugar, baking powder, and salt for the muffin batter.

4. Combine Wet Ingredients:

- In a separate bowl, whisk together the melted butter, milk, egg, and vanilla extract.

5. Combine Wet and Dry Ingredients:

- Pour the wet ingredients into the dry ingredients and stir until just combined. Do not overmix.

6. Add Raspberries:

- Gently fold in the fresh raspberries into the batter.

7. Fill Muffin Cups:

- Divide the batter equally among the muffin cups, filling each about 2/3 full.

8. Add Streusel Topping:

- Sprinkle the streusel topping over each muffin.

9. Bake:

- Bake in the preheated oven for 18-20 minutes or until a toothpick inserted into the center comes out clean.

10. Cool:

- Allow the muffins to cool in the muffin tin for a few minutes, then transfer them to a wire rack to cool completely.

11. Serve:

- Once cooled, enjoy these delicious Raspberry Streusel Muffins with a cup of tea or coffee.

These muffins are a delightful combination of a tender crumb, sweet raspberries, and a crunchy streusel topping. They make for a perfect breakfast or snack option.

Raspberry White Chocolate Cookies

Ingredients:

- 1 cup unsalted butter, softened
- 1 cup granulated sugar
- 2 large eggs
- 1 teaspoon vanilla extract
- 2 and 1/2 cups all-purpose flour
- 1/2 teaspoon baking soda
- 1/4 teaspoon salt
- 1 cup white chocolate chips
- 1 cup fresh raspberries

Instructions:

1. Preheat Oven:

- Preheat your oven to 350°F (175°C). Line baking sheets with parchment paper.

2. Cream Butter and Sugar:

- In a large mixing bowl, cream together the softened butter and granulated sugar until light and fluffy.

3. Add Eggs and Vanilla:

- Beat in the eggs one at a time, ensuring each is well incorporated. Add the vanilla extract and mix until combined.

4. Combine Dry Ingredients:

- In a separate bowl, whisk together the flour, baking soda, and salt.

5. Mix Wet and Dry Ingredients:

- Gradually add the dry ingredients to the wet ingredients, mixing until just combined. Do not overmix.

6. Add White Chocolate and Raspberries:

- Gently fold in the white chocolate chips and fresh raspberries into the cookie dough.

7. Scoop Cookies:

- Using a cookie scoop or tablespoon, drop rounded dough onto the prepared baking sheets, spacing them about 2 inches apart.

8. Bake:

- Bake in the preheated oven for 10-12 minutes or until the edges are golden brown.

9. Cool:

- Allow the cookies to cool on the baking sheets for a few minutes before transferring them to a wire rack to cool completely.

10. Serve:

- Once cooled, serve these delightful Raspberry White Chocolate Cookies and enjoy!

These cookies are a perfect blend of sweet white chocolate and tart raspberries, creating a deliciously balanced treat. They are soft, chewy, and bursting with flavor. Perfect for any occasion or as a delightful addition to your cookie jar!

Raspberry Swirl Brownies

Ingredients:

For the Brownie Batter:

- 1 cup (2 sticks) unsalted butter
- 2 cups granulated sugar
- 4 large eggs
- 1 teaspoon vanilla extract
- 1 cup all-purpose flour
- 1/2 cup cocoa powder
- 1/4 teaspoon salt

For the Raspberry Swirl:

- 1 cup fresh raspberries
- 1/4 cup granulated sugar
- 1 tablespoon water

Instructions:

1. Preheat Oven:

- Preheat your oven to 350°F (175°C). Grease and line a baking pan with parchment paper, leaving an overhang on the sides for easy removal.

2. Prepare Raspberry Swirl:

- In a small saucepan, combine the fresh raspberries, granulated sugar, and water. Cook over medium heat, stirring and mashing the raspberries with a spoon until they break down into a sauce. Simmer for about 5-7 minutes until the mixture thickens slightly. Remove from heat and strain through a fine-mesh sieve to remove seeds. Set aside.

3. Make Brownie Batter:

- In a medium saucepan, melt the butter over low heat. Remove from heat and stir in the sugar until well combined. Add the eggs, one at a time, beating well after each addition. Stir in the vanilla extract.
- In a separate bowl, sift together the flour, cocoa powder, and salt. Add the dry ingredients to the wet ingredients, stirring until just combined.

4. Assemble Brownies:

- Pour the brownie batter into the prepared baking pan. Drop spoonfuls of the raspberry sauce onto the brownie batter. Use a knife or toothpick to swirl the raspberry sauce into the brownie batter, creating a marbled effect.

5. Bake:

- Bake in the preheated oven for 25-30 minutes or until a toothpick inserted into the center comes out with a few moist crumbs. Be careful not to overbake.

6. Cool:

- Allow the brownies to cool completely in the pan on a wire rack.

7. Serve:

- Once cooled, lift the brownies out of the pan using the parchment paper overhang. Cut into squares and serve.

Enjoy these decadent Raspberry Swirl Brownies with a perfect balance of rich chocolate and fruity raspberry flavor!

Raspberry Lemon Bars

Ingredients:

For the Crust:

- 1 cup unsalted butter, softened
- 1/2 cup granulated sugar
- 2 cups all-purpose flour
- 1/4 teaspoon salt

For the Raspberry Lemon Filling:

- 1 1/2 cups fresh raspberries
- 1/4 cup granulated sugar
- Zest of 1 lemon
- 1/4 cup fresh lemon juice
- 4 large eggs
- 1 1/2 cups granulated sugar
- 1/4 cup all-purpose flour
- Powdered sugar, for dusting (optional)

Instructions:

1. Preheat Oven:

- Preheat your oven to 350°F (175°C). Grease a 9x13-inch baking pan or line it with parchment paper, leaving an overhang on the sides for easy removal.

2. Make the Crust:

- In a large bowl, cream together the softened butter and granulated sugar until light and fluffy. Add the flour and salt, mixing until just combined. Press the mixture evenly into the bottom of the prepared baking pan.

3. Bake the Crust:

- Bake the crust in the preheated oven for 15-18 minutes or until it's lightly golden. Remove from the oven and let it cool slightly.

4. Prepare Raspberry Layer:

- In a small saucepan, combine the fresh raspberries and 1/4 cup granulated sugar. Cook over medium heat, stirring and mashing the raspberries, until the mixture thickens and becomes syrupy. Remove from heat and strain through a fine-mesh sieve to remove seeds. Set aside.

5. Make Lemon Filling:

- In a medium bowl, whisk together the lemon zest, lemon juice, eggs, granulated sugar, and flour until well combined.

6. Assemble and Bake:

- Pour the lemon filling over the partially baked crust. Drop spoonfuls of the raspberry sauce onto the lemon filling. Use a knife or toothpick to swirl the raspberry sauce into the lemon filling, creating a marbled effect.
- Bake in the preheated oven for 25-30 minutes or until the edges are set, and the center is just slightly jiggly.

7. Cool and Chill:

- Allow the bars to cool completely in the pan on a wire rack. Once cooled, refrigerate for at least 2 hours to set.

8. Serve:

- Lift the bars out of the pan using the parchment paper overhang. Dust with powdered sugar if desired, then cut into squares. Serve and enjoy!

These Raspberry Lemon Bars are a delightful combination of sweet and tart, making them a perfect treat for any occasion.

Ice Cream and Frozen Treats:

Raspberry Swirl Ice Cream

Ingredients:

For the Raspberry Swirl:

- 1 1/2 cups fresh or frozen raspberries
- 1/4 cup granulated sugar
- 1 tablespoon lemon juice

For the Ice Cream Base:

- 2 cups heavy cream
- 1 cup whole milk
- 3/4 cup granulated sugar
- 1 tablespoon pure vanilla extract

Instructions:

1. Prepare Raspberry Swirl:

- In a saucepan, combine the raspberries, sugar, and lemon juice. Cook over medium heat, stirring occasionally, until the raspberries break down and the mixture thickens (about 10-15 minutes).
- Remove from heat and strain the mixture through a fine-mesh sieve to remove the seeds. Allow the raspberry sauce to cool completely.

2. Make Ice Cream Base:

- In a separate bowl, whisk together the heavy cream, whole milk, sugar, and vanilla extract until the sugar is dissolved.

3. Chill Mixture:

- Cover the mixture and refrigerate for at least 2 hours or overnight to chill thoroughly.

4. Churn Ice Cream:

- Pour the chilled ice cream base into an ice cream maker and churn according to the manufacturer's instructions until it reaches a soft-serve consistency.

5. Layer with Raspberry Swirl:

- Transfer a layer of the churned ice cream into a lidded container. Spoon some of the raspberry swirl on top. Repeat layers, finishing with a raspberry swirl layer on top.

6. Swirl and Freeze:

- Use a knife or a skewer to gently swirl the raspberry sauce into the ice cream, creating a marbled effect.
- Cover the container with a lid and freeze the ice cream for at least 4 hours or until firm.

7. Serve:

- Scoop the Raspberry Swirl Ice Cream into bowls or cones. Garnish with fresh raspberries if desired.

Enjoy the delightful combination of creamy vanilla ice cream and the sweet-tart swirl of raspberry in this homemade treat!

Chocolate Raspberry Popsicles

Ingredients:

- 1 cup fresh raspberries
- 2 tablespoons granulated sugar
- 1 teaspoon lemon juice
- 1 cup chocolate chips
- 2 tablespoons coconut oil
- 1 cup plain Greek yogurt
- 1/2 cup milk (any type you prefer)
- 1 teaspoon vanilla extract

Instructions:

1. Raspberry Puree:

- In a blender or food processor, blend the fresh raspberries, sugar, and lemon juice until smooth. Strain the mixture through a fine-mesh sieve to remove the seeds. Set aside.

2. Melt Chocolate:

- In a microwave-safe bowl, melt the chocolate chips and coconut oil in 20-second intervals, stirring in between, until smooth. Let it cool slightly.

3. Prepare Yogurt Mixture:

- In another bowl, whisk together the Greek yogurt, milk, and vanilla extract until well combined.

4. Layering:

- Start by spooning a layer of the raspberry puree into popsicle molds.
- Follow with a layer of the melted chocolate.
- Add a layer of the yogurt mixture.
- Repeat the layers until the molds are filled, ending with a raspberry puree layer on top.

5. Swirl and Freeze:

- Use a skewer or popsicle stick to gently swirl the layers in each mold for a marbled effect.
- Insert popsicle sticks into each mold.
- Freeze the popsicles for at least 4-6 hours or until fully set.

6. Unmold and Enjoy:

- Once the popsicles are frozen, run the molds under warm water for a few seconds to loosen the popsicles.
- Gently pull the popsicles out of the molds.
- Enjoy your delicious Chocolate Raspberry Popsicles!

These popsicles are a delightful combination of rich chocolate and the bright, fruity flavor of raspberries – a perfect frozen treat for a hot day!

Raspberry Frozen Yogurt

Ingredients:

- 2 cups fresh or frozen raspberries
- 1/2 cup granulated sugar (adjust according to your sweetness preference)
- 2 cups plain Greek yogurt
- 1 tablespoon lemon juice
- 1 teaspoon vanilla extract

Instructions:

Prepare Raspberries:
- If using fresh raspberries, wash them thoroughly. If using frozen raspberries, allow them to thaw slightly.
- In a blender or food processor, puree the raspberries until smooth.

Strain Raspberry Puree:
- If you prefer a smoother texture, you can strain the raspberry puree through a fine-mesh sieve to remove the seeds. This step is optional.

Mix Ingredients:
- In a bowl, combine the raspberry puree, Greek yogurt, granulated sugar, lemon juice, and vanilla extract. Mix well until the sugar is completely dissolved.

Chill Mixture:
- Cover the bowl and refrigerate the mixture for at least 2 hours, allowing the flavors to meld and the mixture to chill.

Churn in Ice Cream Maker:
- Transfer the chilled mixture to your ice cream maker and churn according to the manufacturer's instructions. This usually takes about 15-20 minutes.

Freeze:
- Once the frozen yogurt reaches a soft-serve consistency, you can enjoy it immediately or transfer it to an airtight container and freeze for an additional 2-3 hours for a firmer texture.

Serve and Enjoy:
- Scoop the raspberry frozen yogurt into bowls or cones.
- Garnish with fresh raspberries or a mint sprig if desired.

Optional: Swirl in Extras:

- For added texture and flavor, you can swirl in extras like chocolate chips, chopped nuts, or additional fruit during the last few minutes of churning.

Note:
- If you don't have an ice cream maker, you can pour the mixture into a shallow dish, cover it, and freeze it. Every 30 minutes, stir the mixture with a fork to break up ice crystals until it reaches the desired consistency.

Enjoy your homemade Raspberry Frozen Yogurt!

Raspberry Sorbet Floats

Ingredients:

- Raspberry sorbet
- Lemon-lime soda (or sparkling water for a less sweet option)
- Fresh raspberries (for garnish)
- Mint leaves (optional, for garnish)

Instructions:

Scoop Raspberry Sorbet:
- Using an ice cream scoop, place a few scoops of raspberry sorbet into serving glasses. The amount depends on the size of your glasses.

Pour Soda:
- Slowly pour lemon-lime soda or sparkling water over the raspberry sorbet. The fizziness will create a frothy, refreshing float.

Garnish:
- Garnish the floats with a few fresh raspberries on top.

Add Mint Leaves (Optional):
- For a burst of freshness, add mint leaves to the floats. This is optional but adds a lovely aroma.

Serve Immediately:
- Serve the raspberry sorbet floats immediately while they are fizzy and refreshing.

Enjoy:
- Grab a straw and enjoy the delightful combination of tangy raspberry sorbet and bubbly soda.

These Raspberry Sorbet Floats are not only delicious but also visually appealing, making them perfect for a hot day or as a delightful dessert for any occasion. Feel free to get creative and customize them with your favorite soda or sparkling water!

Raspberry Ice Cream Sandwiches

Ingredients:

- Raspberry ice cream (store-bought or homemade)
- Chocolate chip cookies (store-bought or homemade)

Instructions:

Prepare Cookies (if homemade):
- If you're making your own cookies, bake a batch of chocolate chip cookies according to your favorite recipe. Make sure to let them cool completely before assembling the ice cream sandwiches.

Softened Ice Cream:
- Take the raspberry ice cream out of the freezer and let it soften slightly at room temperature. Softened ice cream is easier to work with.

Assemble the Ice Cream Sandwiches:
- Match up pairs of cookies that are similar in size.
- On the flat side of one cookie, place a scoop of softened raspberry ice cream.

Create Sandwiches:
- Gently press a second cookie on top of the ice cream to create a sandwich. Press down just enough to spread the ice cream to the edges.

Smooth Edges (Optional):
- If desired, use a knife or a spoon to smooth the edges of the ice cream.

Wrap or Serve Immediately:
- You can either serve the ice cream sandwiches immediately or wrap them individually in plastic wrap and place them in the freezer for later.

Freeze (Optional):
- If you have time, you can freeze the assembled ice cream sandwiches for a couple of hours to firm up the ice cream.

Enjoy:
- Once the ice cream sandwiches are firm, they are ready to be enjoyed! Simply unwrap and indulge.

These Raspberry Ice Cream Sandwiches are a delicious and fun treat, perfect for cooling down on a hot day or as a delightful dessert for any occasion. Feel free to get creative with different cookie and ice cream flavors!

Jams and Preserves:

Homemade Raspberry Jam

Ingredients:

- 4 cups fresh raspberries
- 3 cups granulated sugar
- 1 tablespoon lemon juice

Instructions:

Prepare Jars:
- Wash the jars and lids in hot, soapy water. Rinse well and let them air dry. Sterilize the jars by placing them in a boiling water bath for 10 minutes.

Prepare Raspberries:
- Rinse the raspberries under cold water and gently pat them dry with a paper towel.

Combine Ingredients:
- In a large, heavy-bottomed pot, combine the raspberries, sugar, and lemon juice.

Mash Raspberries:
- Use a potato masher or the back of a spoon to gently mash the raspberries, breaking them down and releasing their juices.

Cook the Jam:
- Bring the raspberry mixture to a boil over medium-high heat, stirring frequently. Skim off any foam that rises to the surface.

Check for Gel Point:
- To check for the gel point, place a small plate in the freezer. Spoon a small amount of the jam onto the cold plate, let it sit for a minute, then push the edge of the jam with your finger. If it wrinkles and holds its shape, the jam is ready.

Remove from Heat:
- Once the jam reaches the desired consistency, remove it from the heat.

Fill Jars:
- Carefully ladle the hot jam into the prepared, sterilized jars, leaving about 1/4-inch headspace.

Seal Jars:

- Wipe the rims of the jars with a clean, damp cloth to remove any residue. Place the sterilized lids on the jars and screw on the metal bands until fingertip-tight.

Process Jars (Optional):
- Process the jars in a boiling water bath for 10 minutes to ensure they are sealed properly.

Cool and Store:
- Allow the jars to cool to room temperature. Check the seals by pressing down on the center of each lid; if it doesn't pop back, the jar is sealed. Store sealed jars in a cool, dark place.

Enjoy:
- Once the jam has cooled and set, it's ready to be enjoyed on toast, scones, or as a delicious topping for desserts.

This homemade Raspberry Jam is a delightful way to preserve the fresh, fruity flavor of raspberries. Enjoy the taste of summer all year round!

Raspberry Balsamic Reduction

Ingredients:

- 4 cups fresh raspberries
- 3 cups granulated sugar
- 1 tablespoon lemon juice

Instructions:

Prepare Jars:
- Wash the jars and lids in hot, soapy water. Rinse well and let them air dry. Sterilize the jars by placing them in a boiling water bath for 10 minutes.

Prepare Raspberries:
- Rinse the raspberries under cold water and gently pat them dry with a paper towel.

Combine Ingredients:
- In a large, heavy-bottomed pot, combine the raspberries, sugar, and lemon juice.

Mash Raspberries:
- Use a potato masher or the back of a spoon to gently mash the raspberries, breaking them down and releasing their juices.

Cook the Jam:
- Bring the raspberry mixture to a boil over medium-high heat, stirring frequently. Skim off any foam that rises to the surface.

Check for Gel Point:
- To check for the gel point, place a small plate in the freezer. Spoon a small amount of the jam onto the cold plate, let it sit for a minute, then push the edge of the jam with your finger. If it wrinkles and holds its shape, the jam is ready.

Remove from Heat:
- Once the jam reaches the desired consistency, remove it from the heat.

Fill Jars:
- Carefully ladle the hot jam into the prepared, sterilized jars, leaving about 1/4-inch headspace.

Seal Jars:

- Wipe the rims of the jars with a clean, damp cloth to remove any residue. Place the sterilized lids on the jars and screw on the metal bands until fingertip-tight.

Process Jars (Optional):
- Process the jars in a boiling water bath for 10 minutes to ensure they are sealed properly.

Cool and Store:
- Allow the jars to cool to room temperature. Check the seals by pressing down on the center of each lid; if it doesn't pop back, the jar is sealed. Store sealed jars in a cool, dark place.

Enjoy:
- Once the jam has cooled and set, it's ready to be enjoyed on toast, scones, or as a delicious topping for desserts.

This homemade Raspberry Jam is a delightful way to preserve the fresh, fruity flavor of raspberries. Enjoy the taste of summer all year round!

Spicy Raspberry Sauce

Ingredients:

- 2 cups fresh raspberries
- 1/2 cup granulated sugar
- 1 tablespoon lemon juice
- 1 teaspoon red pepper flakes (adjust to taste)
- Pinch of salt

Instructions:

Prepare Raspberries:
- Rinse the raspberries under cold water and pat them dry with a paper towel.

Combine Ingredients:
- In a saucepan, combine the raspberries, sugar, lemon juice, red pepper flakes, and a pinch of salt.

Cook over Medium Heat:
- Place the saucepan over medium heat and bring the mixture to a simmer, stirring frequently to dissolve the sugar.

Simmer:
- Once it reaches a simmer, reduce the heat to low and let it simmer for 10-15 minutes, or until the raspberries break down and the sauce thickens.

Adjust Spiciness:
- Taste the sauce and adjust the level of spiciness by adding more red pepper flakes if desired.

Strain (Optional):
- If you prefer a smoother sauce, you can strain the mixture through a fine-mesh sieve to remove seeds. Use the back of a spoon to press the sauce through, leaving the seeds behind.

Cool:
- Allow the sauce to cool to room temperature.

Store:
- Transfer the spicy raspberry sauce to a jar or airtight container and refrigerate. It will continue to thicken as it cools.

Serve:
- Use the spicy raspberry sauce as a condiment for grilled meats, as a topping for desserts, or even as a dipping sauce.

This Spicy Raspberry Sauce adds a kick to the sweet and tart flavor of raspberries, making it a versatile and delicious addition to a variety of dishes. Enjoy!

Raspberry Lemon Curd

Ingredients:

- 1 cup fresh raspberries
- 1 cup granulated sugar
- Zest of 2 lemons
- 1/2 cup freshly squeezed lemon juice (about 3-4 lemons)
- 4 large eggs
- 1/2 cup unsalted butter, cubed

Instructions:

Prepare Raspberries:
- Rinse the raspberries and set them aside.

Double Boiler Setup:
- Set up a double boiler by placing a heatproof bowl over a pot of simmering water. Make sure the bottom of the bowl doesn't touch the water.

Combine Ingredients:
- In the heatproof bowl, whisk together the sugar, lemon zest, lemon juice, and eggs.

Cooking:
- Whisk the mixture continuously over medium heat until it starts to thicken. This will take about 8-10 minutes.

Add Butter:
- Once the mixture has thickened, add the cubed butter and continue whisking until the butter is fully melted and the curd is smooth.

Add Raspberries:
- Remove the bowl from heat and gently fold in the fresh raspberries. The heat from the curd will slightly soften the raspberries.

Strain (Optional):
- If you prefer a smoother curd, you can strain it through a fine-mesh sieve to remove the raspberry seeds. Use the back of a spoon to press the curd through the sieve.

Cool:
- Let the raspberry lemon curd cool to room temperature.

Refrigerate:

- Transfer the curd to a jar or airtight container and refrigerate for at least 2 hours or until it's chilled.

Serve:
- Use the raspberry lemon curd as a topping for scones, pancakes, toast, or as a filling for pastries and cakes.

This Raspberry Lemon Curd combines the bright citrusy flavor of lemons with the sweetness of raspberries, creating a luscious and vibrant spread that's perfect for various desserts and breakfast treats. Enjoy!

Raspberry Compote

Ingredients:

- 2 cups fresh raspberries
- 1/2 cup granulated sugar
- 1 tablespoon lemon juice
- 1 teaspoon cornstarch (optional, for thickening)

Instructions:

Combine Ingredients:
- In a saucepan, combine the fresh raspberries, granulated sugar, and lemon juice.

Cook Over Medium Heat:
- Place the saucepan over medium heat and bring the mixture to a gentle boil. Stir occasionally to help dissolve the sugar.

Simmer:
- Reduce the heat to low and let the mixture simmer for about 8-10 minutes. The raspberries will break down, and the mixture will thicken slightly.

Optional Thickening:
- If you prefer a thicker compote, you can mix 1 teaspoon of cornstarch with a little water to create a slurry. Stir the slurry into the raspberry mixture and simmer for an additional 2-3 minutes until thickened.

Cool:
- Remove the saucepan from heat and let the raspberry compote cool to room temperature.

Serve or Store:
- Use the raspberry compote as a topping for desserts, pancakes, waffles, ice cream, or yogurt. Store any leftovers in an airtight container in the refrigerator.

This Raspberry Compote is a versatile and delicious addition to many dishes, providing a burst of sweet and tart flavor. Enjoy!

www.ingramcontent.com/pod-product-compliance
Lightning Source LLC
LaVergne TN
LVHW061946070526
838199LV00060B/3996